A Kid's Guide to Drawing America™

How to Draw
New Hampshire's
Sights and Symbols

Stephanie True Peters

The Rosen Publishing Group's
PowerKids Press™
New York

Published in 2002 by The Rosen Publishing Group, Inc.
29 East 21st Street, New York, NY 10010

First Edition

Editor: Jannell Khu
Book Design: Kim Sonsky
Layout Design: Nick Scaccia

Illustration Credits: Emily Muschinske
Photo Credits: p. 7 © David Muench/CORBIS; pp. 12, 14 © One Mile Up, Incorporated; p. 16 © Eric And David Hosking/CORBIS; p. 18 © Steve Austin; Papilio/CORBIS; p. 20 © Tim Zurowski/CORBIS; p. 22 © Dick Hamilton Photo; p. 24 © Joe McDonald/CORBIS; p. 26 © Lee Snider; Lee Snider/CORBIS; p. 28 © Joseph Sohm; ChromoSohm Inc./CORBIS.

Peters, Stephanie True, 1965–
How to draw New Hampshire's sights and symbols / Stephanie T. Peters.
p. cm. — (A kid's guide to drawing America)
Includes index.
Summary: This book explains how to draw some of New Hampshire's sights and symbols, including the state seal, the official flower, and the Old Man of the Mountain, New Hampshire's most famous landmark.
  ISBN 0-8239-6085-4
1. Emblems, State—New Hampshire—Juvenile literature 2. New Hampshire—
In art—Juvenile literature 3. Drawing—Technique—Juvenile literature
[1. Emblems, State—New Hampshire 2. New Hampshire 3. Drawing—
Technique] I. Title II. Series
  2002
  743'.8'99742—dc21

Manufactured in the United States of America

CONTENTS

Let's Draw New Hampshire

New Hampshire is located in the northeastern corner of the United States, called New England. New Hampshire has a lot of breathtaking scenery. One of the country's most famous natural rock formations, the Old Man of the Mountain, is in the White Mountains. The White Mountains are also home to Mount Washington, the highest peak in the Northeast at 6,288 feet (1,916.5 m) above sea level. Another natural wonder found in the White Mountains is the Flume. This natural waterway has carved a gorge through the rock over time. One way to see some of these magnificent sights is to go to Bretton Woods, New Hampshire, and to catch a ride on the Mount Washington Cog Railway. This railway was the first mountain-climbing railway in the world and is a National Historic Engineering Landmark.

New Hampshire has had a rich political tradition since 1629, when people came from England and settled in the area. On June 21, 1788, New Hampshire became the ninth state to approve the Constitution of the United States. The fourteenth president of the United States, Franklin Pierce, was born and raised in New Hampshire. New Hampshire was also the birthplace of Daniel Webster, a politician who protested the Civil War. He fought long and hard for the preservation of the Union. This book will take you on a grand tour of New Hampshire and will show you how to draw some of its sights and symbols. Each drawing is broken down into simple steps. There are directions under each step. When a new step is added, it is shown in red. Before you start, find a comfortable place to draw and gather the following supplies:

- A sketch pad
- An eraser
- A number 2 pencil
- A pencil sharpener

These are some of the shapes and drawing terms you need to know to draw New Hampshire's sights and symbols:

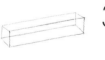 3-D box

 Shading

Almond shape

 Squiggle

—— Horizontal line

 Teardrop

Oval

| Vertical line

Rectangle

Wavy line

The Granite State

New Hampshire's official nickname is the Granite State because this high-quality stone is quarried there. New Hampshire is also known as the Primary State because it has been the site of the first U.S. presidential primary every election year since 1920. A primary is an election to decide who will be the presidential candidates. The winner of New Hampshire's primary is often elected to be the U.S. president. Since 1952, almost every winner of the New Hampshire primary has been elected president. A library of documents about the New Hampshire primary is located in Concord, the state's capital.

Concord was the home of Christa McAuliffe, a social studies teacher chosen by the National Aeronautics and Space Administration (NASA) to be the first private citizen and teacher in space. McAuliffe never fulfilled her dream. She was killed when the space shuttle *Challenger* exploded on January 28, 1986, 73 seconds after takeoff. Today a planetarium in Concord is named for this brave woman.

New Hampshire is known for its granite. If you visit Franconia Notch State Park, you can see this scenic spot where water rushes over granite rocks.

Artist in New Hampshire

Edward Hill was born in 1843, in England. He moved to the United States when he was still a boy. Many people think Hill learned how to paint from his older brother, who was also an artist. Hill painted natural landscapes, such as mountains, valleys, lakes, and forests, in a realistic way. His best-known paintings are of New Hampshire's White Mountains. He used oil paints on canvas. Hill's landscape *Presidential Range* captures the awesome peaks of the White Mountains in north-central New Hampshire. Clouds sweep through the blue sky above the

Edward Hill

Franconia Notch is a pencil-on-paper sketch. Hill drew this sketch between 1870 and 1899.

mountains while picture-perfect trees below seem to bend in the wind. Edward Hill spent many years hiking through the areas he painted. He made sketches of scenes that he planned to paint. Considering New Hampshire's often-cold temperatures, it's not surprising that he chose to paint in a studio from sketches and from photos rather than paint on location! Many people who bought Hill's paintings were tourists. They wanted to take home pictures of the magnificent landscapes. Edward Hill moved to the Pacific Northwest in 1911. He lived there until he passed away in 1923.

Courtesy of New Hampshire Historical Society

Hill painted *Presidential Range* in 1886. It measures 30" x 50" (76 cm x 127 cm) and is an oil-on-canvas painting.

Map of New Hampshire

Map of the Continental United States

New Hampshire can be divided into three topographical regions. The White Mountains region has the peaks of the Presidential Range, as well as the scenic Pinkham, Crawford, and Franconia Notches. South of the White Mountains is the Upland region. This region has farmlands, rivers, lakes, and forests. The Coastal Lowlands region has sandy beaches. Four islands of the nine Isles of Shoals are located in this region. New Hampshire is bordered by Canada to the north, Maine to the northeast, the Atlantic Ocean to the southeast, Massachusetts to the south, and Vermont to the west. The climate ranges from hot, humid summers to cold, snowy winters.

1

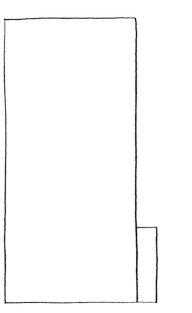

Draw a large rectangle and a smaller rectangle. These shapes are guides to help you draw the state of New Hampshire. If you draw the shapes lightly, it will be easier to erase them later.

2

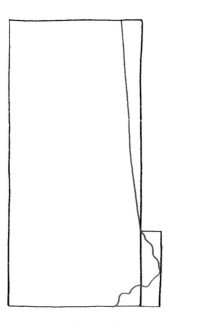

Draw a slanted line down the right side of the larger rectangle. Next use the small rectangle on the bottom right to draw a wavy bump. You just drew the eastern side of New Hampshire. Good job!

3

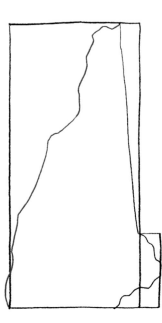

Check out the red highlight. This is the western side of the state. Notice that this line isn't as straight as the eastern side.

4

Erase extra lines.
a. Add a star for Concord, the capital city.
b. Draw a circle for Manchester, the state's most populated city.
c. Draw a triangle for Mount Washington.
d. Draw triangles with two verticle lines below them for White Mountain National Forest.
e. For Lake Winnipesaukee, draw the cloud shape as shown.

11

The State Seal

New Hampshire's first state seal was designed in 1775 and was changed constantly for many years. It never looked the same. This bothered Otis G. Hammond, who was the head of the New Hampshire Historical Society in 1931. At Hammond's suggestion, the government adopted the present seal in 1931. It shows the *Raleigh*, a frigate that was built in Portsmouth, New Hampshire, in 1776. The *Raleigh* was one of the first warships built at the start of the American Revolution. It was the first ship to carry the early American flag into battle. The seal shows the *Raleigh* resting on stocks, a framework that holds a ship while it is being built or repaired. This image shows that  Portsmouth was a major shipbuilding town. Near the bow of the ship is a granite boulder, the state rock.

1

You will draw the seal's central image, the boat. Begin with a circle.

2

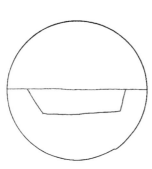

Draw a horizontal line across the circle. Add a rectangular shape underneath it. This will be the outline of the boat.

3

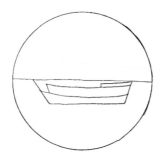

Make horizontal and vertical lines to create the three sections of the boat.

4

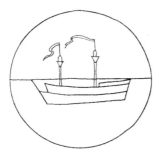

Add lookout towers, flagpoles, and flags. To make the flags appear to blow in the wind, draw them using long, thin, curved lines.

5

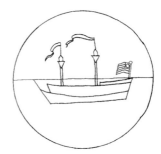

Draw the version of the American flag flown during the American Revolution.

6

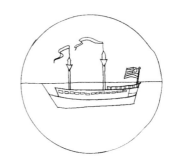

Add railing to the boat's top section. In the middle section, draw a row of small windows and one large window at the far right.

7

Draw lines that connect the tower to the boat. Add detail to the large window. Draw the stocks.

8

Erase extra lines. Shade the boat, and you are done!

13

The State Flag

If you see New Hampshire's state flag next to the state seal, you might think you're seeing double! That's because the seal and the flag are almost identical. The state flag was created in 1909, then was changed in 1931 to match the current state seal. The background of the flag is blue. The state seal is centered in the middle. Laurel leaves and nine stars surround the seal. The stars show that New Hampshire was the ninth state to join the Union. Before 1909, New Hampshire used regimental flags to represent the state. Regimental flags stood for the different military units of New Hampshire. These flags can still be seen in the Hall of Flags, found in New Hampshire's capitol building in Concord.

1

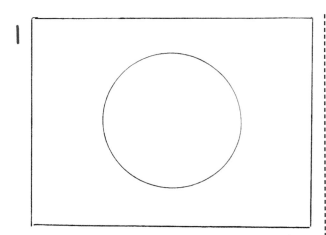

Begin with a rectangle. Add a circle in the center.

2

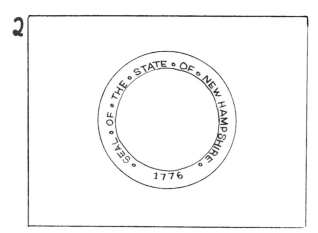

Draw a smaller circle inside the larger one. Write the words "SEAL OF THE STATE OF NEW HAMPSHIRE" between the two circles. Next write 1776 in the bottom center of the two circles. Notice that small dots separate each word and the date.

3

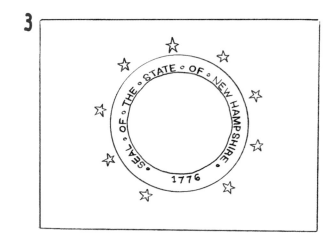

Add nine stars outside the circles. Leave enough space between the stars for the design in the next step.

4

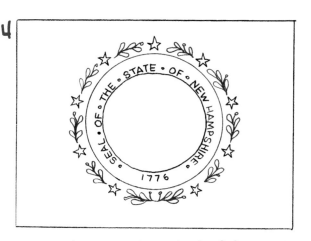

Between the stars, draw the leaf design. Start at the bottom of the circle. Draw a curved line and add six teardrop-shaped leaves. Then add four little lines with small circles on top. Notice the other eight leaf designs have four teardrop-shaped leaves.

5

Add the state seal's boat, which was drawn on page 13.

The Purple Lilac

In 1919, two sisters, Marietta C. Wright and Josephine A. Joslin, suggested the purple lilac for New Hampshire's official state flower. State representative Charles B. Drake supported the idea. Others in the government wanted the apple blossom, because it would represent the state's apple industry. There was concern that if the apple blossom was chosen, people would start picking the popular flower. Without any blossoms left on the trees, there wouldn't be apples in the fall! In the end, the purple lilac won instead of the apple blossom. It also was chosen instead of the evening primrose, the buttercup, and the purple aster. On March 28, 1919, the purple lilac was adopted as New Hampshire's official state flower.

1

Begin with two teardrop shapes. Make the right one thinner than the one on the left. These will be the leaves of the lilac.

2

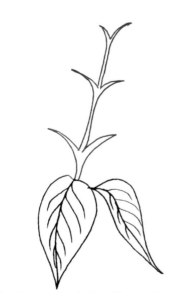

Curve the long leaf's top. Add veins in the leaves. First draw lines down the leaves' middles, then add curved lines on either side.

3

Add the thick stem of the lilac. The small, purple flowers grow from this stem.

4

Add a rounded cloud shape around the stem. Notice that the cloud shape looks like the outline of a snowman.

5

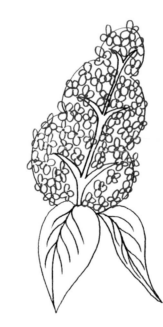

Fill this shape with lilac flowers. Each flower is small and has four circular petals.

The White Birch

The white birch is native to New Hampshire. It can grow up to 80 feet (24 m) tall and has broad, oval leaves on short branches. The most noticeable feature of the white birch is its creamy white bark. The bark can be peeled back in paperlike strips. Native Americans used the bark for paper. They also used it to make canoes. This is why the white birch is sometimes called the paper birch or the canoe birch. Native Americans tapped the tree to get its sap. The sap was boiled down to a sticky syrup, which was used to sweeten tea and to make medicine. In 1947, state senator J. Guy Smart proposed the white birch as the state tree. On May 22, 1947, the white birch became the official state tree of New Hampshire.

1

Begin with a tall, thin trunk. Then add some thin branches that reach upward.

2

Next create the scarred, rough look of the white birch bark. To do this, first lightly shade the tree, then press down on your pencil to darken the areas as shown.

3

Create a fluffy outline around the branches. This is a guide to help you draw the tree leaves.

4

Add a lot of leaves. Birch leaves are shaped like ovals. Good job!

The Purple Finch

In 1957, here was a debate between Representative Doris M. Spollett, who wanted the New Hampshire hen to be the state bird, and Representative Robert S. Monahan, who suggested the purple finch. On April 25, 1957, the finch won the vote and became the state bird. Purple finches are not purple! Males are reddish in color, and females are brownish with white streaks. Purple finches are small birds with short, cone-shaped beaks and V-shaped tails. Both males and females have white bellies. The population has declined in recent years, because other birds compete with the purple finch for food and for nesting areas. Purple finches can be found throughout the forests in New Hampshire.

1

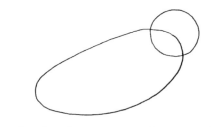

For the body, draw an oval. Next draw a circle for the head.

2

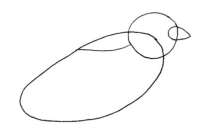

Add the top layer of the wing and a teardrop-shaped beak.

3

Draw more wing layers. First draw a wavy line, then add a straight line underneath it.

4

Add the tail feather and a small circle for the eye. Shade the eye. Divide the beak in half with a horizontal line.

5

Erase extra lines. When you erase extra lines, pay careful attention to lines that overlap. Add the legs, the feet, and a small branch.

6

Finish the legs and shade the purple finch. Nice work!

The Old Man of the Mountain

The Old Man of the Mountain is New Hampshire's most famous natural landmark. If you stand at just the right spot near Profile Lake in Franconia Notch State Park, you can see a granite stone face high on Profile Mountain. The Old Man may look small when seen from the bottom of the mountain, but he's actually 48 ½ feet (15 m) tall. Two thick layers of granite form his forehead. The three bottom layers make his nose, his upper lip, and his chin. His forehead, his nose, and his chin jut out and make him look stubborn. Many artists, poets, and writers have captured the face on paper and in stories. The famous profile can be found on the state's emblem, state highway signs, and other state symbols.

1

Draw a long curved line. Next add three straight lines to it. This is the basic profile of the Old Man.

2

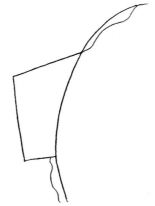

Use the curved line as a guide to draw the edge of the mountain. Use wavy lines to show that the mountain is rocky and uneven.

3

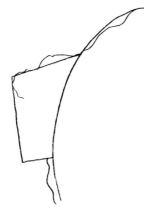

Next begin the outline of the Old Man's head. This is the top of the Old Man's head and his forehead.

4

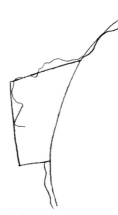

To draw the Old Man's nose, draw two lines as shown in the red highlight.

5

Right under the nose, draw a small straight line. Continue that line two slanted lines, as shown. This is his mouth. Finish this step with another straight line for the chin.

6

Erase extra lines. Look at the above step as a guide and shade some areas lighter than others. Your drawing should look like a man's profile.

The Spotted Newt

The story of how the spotted newt became New Hampshire's state amphibian is one of concern for the environment. From 1983 to 1985, New Hampshire high-school students urged their state government to adopt the newt as a state symbol. They believed the newt could be a powerful symbol of a movement to clean up New Hampshire's polluted air and to protect the newt's natural habitat, the wetlands. Acid rain was destroying the grassy swamps and the ponds in which the newts live. In 1985, New Hampshire's government listened and named the spotted newt the official state amphibian. A young newt is called an eft. Spotted newt efts are bright red with black-bordered, red spots. When they become adults, they turn green and yellow.

1

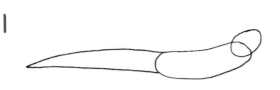

To start draw the three basic shapes of the newt's body. First draw its round head, its hotdog-shaped body, and its long, pointed tail.

2

Draw two small parallel lines near the head. Then draw a small circle and two lines as shown. Near the tail, draw a half oval shape and two curved parallel lines. These are the newt's legs.

3

Begin to draw the newt's feet. Draw two round shapes for its two front feet. For its hind foot, draw a fan shape.

4

Draw the newt's fingers and its toes.

5

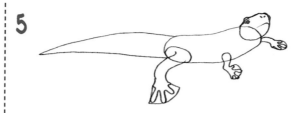

Next draw the newt's eyes, its nose, and its mouth.

6

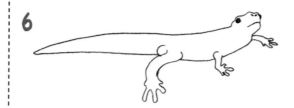

Erase extra lines. Pay extra attention to lines that overlap. After you have erased, your newt should look like the drawing above.

7

First shade the newt. Next draw its spots, and you're done!

Portsmouth Harbor

When Portsmouth was settled in 1623, it was known as Strawbery Banke because of the wild strawberries that covered its hillsides. Portsmouth is the nation's third-oldest city. It was the state capital until 1808, when the capital was moved to Concord. By the 1800s, Portsmouth was famous for its harbor and for shipbuilding. One of the types of ships built in Portsmouth was the clipper ship. Clipper ships were lightweight, swift-moving sailboats used by merchants to move cargo throughout the world. The fastest clipper ship in the world was the *Nightingale*, built at Portsmouth in 1851. Today Portsmouth Harbor is the home of a naval shipyard. The submarine *Albacore* rests where the *Nightingale* might once have floated.

1

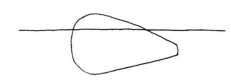

Draw a horizontal line. Next draw a teardrop shape. This is the belly of the ship. The wide part of the teardrop is the front of the ship.

2

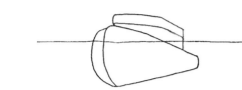

Next draw a curved vertical line on the front of the ship. Draw the first level and the second level on top of the ship.

3

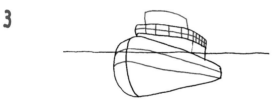

Draw another vertical line in the first level. Draw the rails on the boat's second level. Add the third level of the ship. Draw two horizontal lines on the belly of the ship.

4

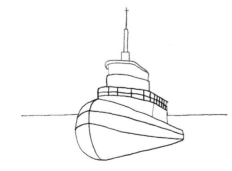

Use four lines to finish the third level of the ship. Next draw the tower stand and the tower on top of the third level.

5

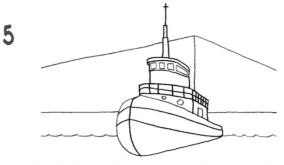

For the harbor, draw a straight vertical line and two diagonal horizontal lines. Draw the windows on the first and third levels of the ship. Use wavy lines for the water.

6

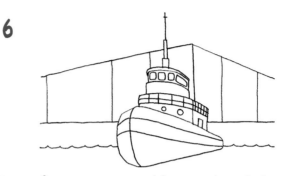

Draw five more vertical lines to break the harbor into a block of buildings.

7

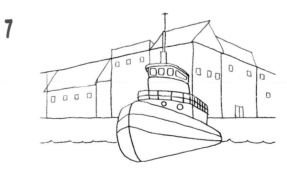

Add rooftops and windows.

8

Add shading and you're done!

New Hampshire's Capitol

Concord became New Hampshire's capital in 1808. The capitol building was made from the state's finest granite. Construction was completed in 1819. Several important laws were created there.

In the 1800s, New Hampshire had many textile mills. Adults and even children as young as ten years old worked difficult and dangerous jobs. They worked many hours and often got hurt on the job because they were tired. In 1847, a law was passed so that the laborers wouldn't have to work more than ten hours each day. In 1871, another law was passed that stated all children had to attend school. This law might have helped some children get out of the mills completely.

1

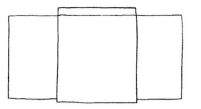

First draw a long rectangle. Next draw another rectangle on top of the first one.

2

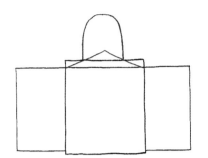

Add a triangle and an arc. The triangle is called a pediment, and the arc is called a dome.

3

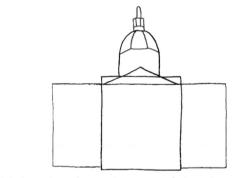

Add the details to the top of the dome.

4

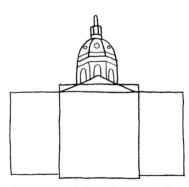

Divide the bottom of the dome with lines. Add round windows in the dome's upper part and arched windows in the dome's lower part.

5

Add horizontal lines to divide the front of the building.

6

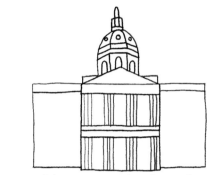

Add vertical lines to make the columns. They support the front of the building.

7

Add rows of arched windows and of square windows. Add a door and a staircase.

8

Shade the capitol. Notice that some areas are shaded darker than others.

29

New Hampshire State Facts

Statehood	June 21, 1788, 9th state
Area	9,304 square miles (24,097 sq km)
Population	1,185,000
Capital	Concord, population, 39,100
Most Populated City	Manchester, population, 106,200
Industries	Tourism, computers, electronics, wood products, banking, education
Agriculture	Forest products, apples, poultry, maple syrup, milk, beef cattle, hay
Nickname	The Granite State
Motto	Live Free Or Die
Mineral	Beryl
Gemstone	Smoky quartz
Rock	Granite
Insect	Ladybug
Animal	White-tailed deer
Amphibian	Spotted newt
Freshwater Fish	Brook trout
Saltwater Fish	Striped bass
Flower	Purple lilac
Wildflower	Pink lady slipper

Glossary

acid rain (A-sid RAYN) Rainwater that is polluted by chemicals in the air.

American Revolution (uh-MER-uh-ken reh-vuh-LOO-shun) Battles that soldiers from the colonies fought against England for freedom.

amphibian (am-FIH-bee-uhn) An animal that lives both in water and on land.

candidate (KAN-dih-dayt) A person hoping to be elected to an official position.

Civil War (SIH-vul WOR) The war fought between the northern and southern states of America from 1861 to 1865.

clipper ship (KLIH-per SHIP) A lightweight, fast-moving sailboat used in the 1800s to move goods.

emblem (EM-bluhm) A picture with a motto.

frigate (FRIH-git) A three-masted sailing ship that carries its guns on a single gun deck.

landscapes (LAND-skayps) Paintings of scenes found in nature, such as mountains, lakes, and beaches.

preservation (preh-zer-VAY-shun) The act of keeping something safe, of protecting.

primary (PRY-mair-ee) An early election held to decide who is going to be president.

proposed (pruh-POHZD) Suggested, planned.

quarried (KWOR-eed) Dug out, mined.

regimental (reh-juh-MEN-tuhl) Military, such as having to do with the army or the navy.

textile mills (TEK-styl MILZ) Factories where cloth is made.

topographical (tah-puh-GRA-fih-kuhl) Referring to a type of map that shows different regions, such as mountains, lakes, and forests.

Index

Web Sites

To find out more about New Hampshire, check out these Web sites:

www.50states.com/newhamps.htm
www.state.nh.us
www.nh.com